PART II

Compiled by Joan Frey Boytim

EASY
SONGS
FOR THE
BEGINNING
SOPRANO
PART II

LABORUM
DULCE
LENIMEN

G. SCHIRMER

Laura Ward, pianist

ISBN 978-1-4234-1213-7

G. SCHIRMER, Inc.

DISTRIBUTED BY
HAL•LEONARD®
CORPORATION
7777 W. BLUEMOUND RD. P.O.BOX 13819 MILWAUKEE, WI 53213

www.schirmer.com
www.halleonard.com

To access companion recorded piano accompaniments online, visit:
www.halleonard.com/mylibrary

Enter Code
4207-0955-6626-9533

If you require a physical CD of the online audio that accompanies this book,
please contact Hal Leonard Corporation at info@halleonard.com

PREFACE

The success of the books in the series *Easy Songs for Beginning Singers* indicates that there is a need for more preparatory literature of this type for middle school and high school singers in early stages of traditional vocal study. Teachers have commented to me that in some colleges these books are even used with very inexperienced freshmen, or with beginning adult singers.

The volumes of *Easy Songs for Beginning Singers—Part II* are at the same level as the original books. They can be used alone or in conjunction with the first set. Based on a teacher's choice of songs, there is no reason that a student could not easily start in *Part II*. Both volumes of *Easy Songs for Beginning Singers* lead very nicely into *The First Book of Solos* series (original set, *Part II*, or *Part III*).

There are 18-20 songs per volume in *Easy Songs—Part II*. A number of the selections have been out of print and will be unfamiliar to some teachers. All the songs chosen are very melodic and should pose no major musical or vocal problems for beginners of all types.

The compilation theory behind these volumes remains basically the same as in the original set. All songs are in English, some in translation, to keep the music easier to learn and comprehend. We have used songs with moderate ranges and tessituras to facilitate the building of technique. The wide variety of music includes folksongs, early show songs, operetta, parlor songs from c. 1900, as well as very easy art songs.

The art song composers include Schubert, Schumann, Franz, Arensky, Rimsky-Korsakov, Grieg, Quilter, Ireland, Head, Hopkinson, Beach and Dougherty. Operetta and vintage popular composers include Kalman, Romberg, Herbert, Berlin and Meyer. Care has been taken to provide the male voices with masculine texts. Some "old chestnuts" which young people may have never experienced include "Glow Worm," "Trees," "The Bells of St. Mary's," "Somewhere a Voice is Calling," and "Because."

My wish is that this set of books provides more options for the novice singer of any age, and helps all of my fellow teachers with the ongoing aim to lead more students into the joys of classical singing. Incidentally, these volumes may also be another source of relaxed and fun material for experienced singers.

Joan Frey Boytim
May, 2006

CONTENTS

The price of this publication includes access to companion recorded piano accompaniments online, for download or streaming, using the unique code found on the title page. Visit **www.halleonard.com/mylibrary** and enter the access code.

to Robin and Aimée Legge

APRIL

William Watson

Roger Quilter
(1877-1953)

Allegro scherzoso e leggiero ♩ = 126

A - pril

A - pril, Laugh thy girl-ish laugh - ter, Then, the mo - ment

poco rit.   *a tempo*

af - ter, Weep thy girl - ish tears._____

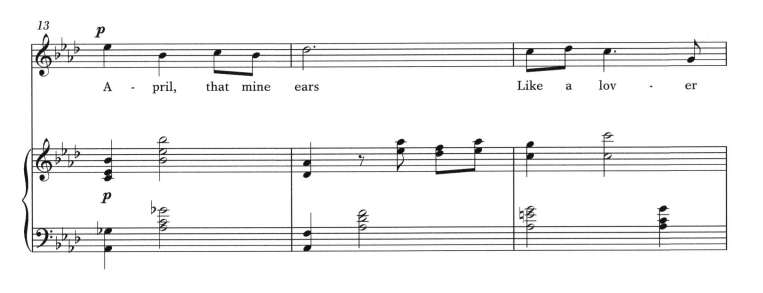

A - pril, that mine ears Like a lov - er

greet - est, If I tell thee, sweet - est, All my hopes and

fears A - pril, A - pril,

Laugh thy gol-den laugh - ter, But, the mo - ment af - ter

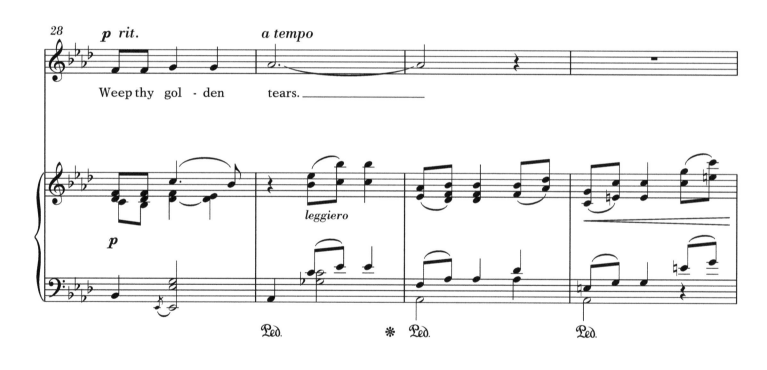

Weep thy gol - den tears._____

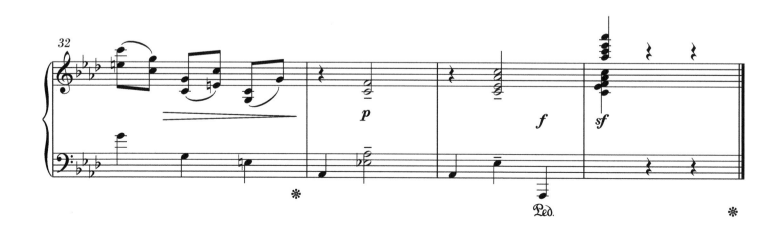

BECAUSE

Edward Teschemacher

Guy d'Hardelot
(1858-1936)

THE BELLS OF ST. MARY'S

Douglas Furber

A. Emmett Adams

Moderately

The

bells of St. Mar - y's, Ah! hear they are call - ing The

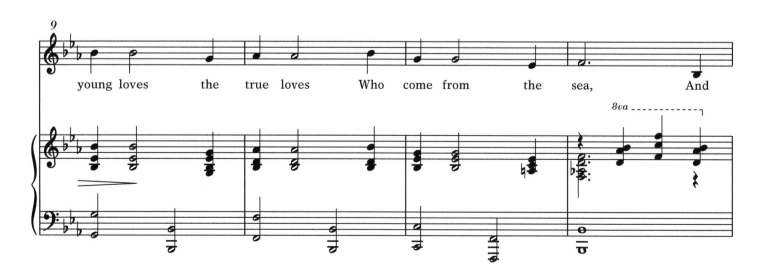

young loves the true loves Who come from the sea, And

CRADLE SONG

Thomas Bailey Aldrich

Reginald De Koven
(1859-1920)

BY THE WATERS OF MINNETONKA

J.M. Cavanass

Thurlow Lieurance
(1878-1963)

FAIRY LULLABY

William Shakespeare

Amy Marcy Cheney Beach
(1867-1944)

Tempo I

FROM THE LAND OF SKY-BLUE WATER

Nelle Richmond Eberhart

Charles Wakefield Cadman
(1881-1946)

* Flageolet Love Call of the Omahas

GLOW WORM

Lilla Cayley Robinson

Paul Lincke
(1866-1946)

Tempo di Gavotte

When the night falls si-lent-ly, ____ the night falls si-lent-ly ____ on for-ests
"Lit - tle glow - worm, tell me pray, ____ oh glow-worm, tell me pray, ____ how did you

dream - ing, Lov - ers wan - der forth to see, ____ they wan-der
kin - dle, Lamps that by the break of day, ____ that by the

forth to see ____ the bright stars gleam - ing; And lest they should
break of day, ____ must fade and dwin - dle?" "Ah this se - cret,

32

HE STOLE MY TENDER HEART AWAY

Early American Song

Harmonized by Samuel Endicott

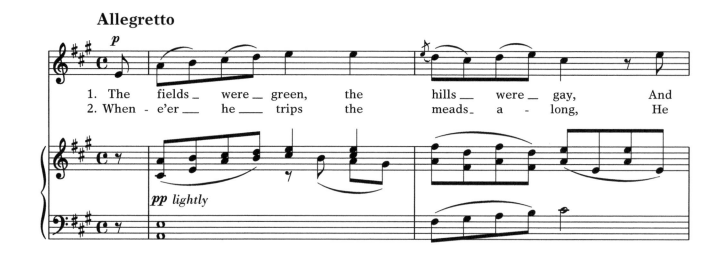

HEDGE-ROSES
(Heidenröslein)

Johann Wolfgang von Goethe
English version by Charles Fonteyn Manney

Franz Schubert
(1797-1828)

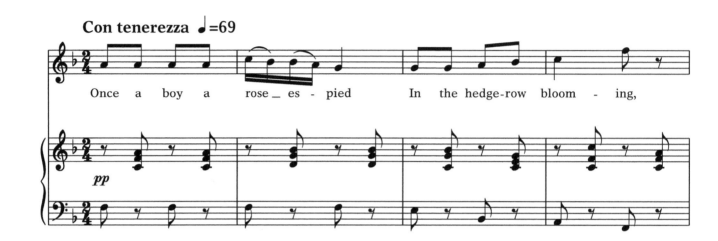

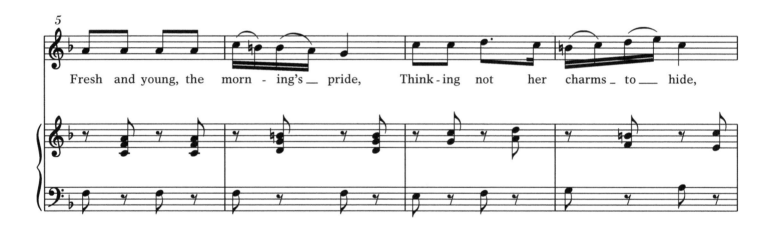

A LITTLE BIT OF HEAVEN

Ernest R. Ball

J. Keirn Brennan
(1873-1948)

IN THE WOODS
(Waldfahrt)

Theodor Körner
English version by John S. Dwight

Robert Franz
(1815-1892)

clear blue sky and the sun's bright beams In wood - lands, cool - ing

wood - lands. The woods, the woods, are the home of

love, The _ birds trill their songs in the boughs a - bove, the flow'rs _ by

twi - light calm - ly calls forth the night, We find our way, __ and

seek __ our rest __ Still the en - chant-ment doth fill our breast Of

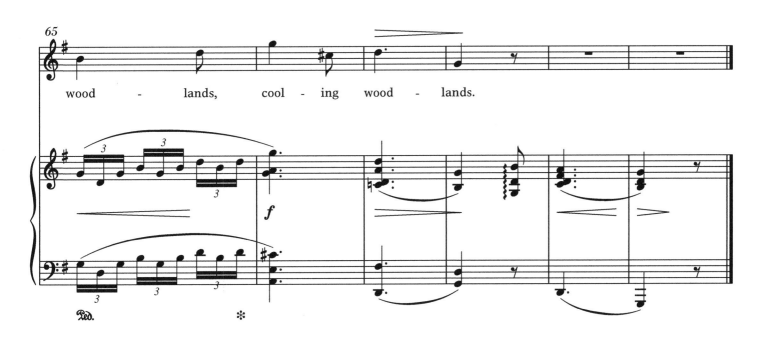

wood - lands, cool - ing wood - lands.

A KISS IN THE DARK

B. G. de Sylva

Victor Herbert
(1859-1924)

dark   But _____ it kin - dled _____ the spark,

The _____ a - wak - 'ning _____ of love's   young

poco accel.   *rit.*

dream!   Oh,   that

molto rit.

dream! _____

THE LITTLE RED LARK

Alfred Perceval Graves

Irish Air
Arranged by William Arms Fisher
(1861-1948)

1. O swan of slen - der - ness Dove of ten - der - ness
2. The dawn is dark to me, Hark, oh, hark to me,

Jew - el of joys __ a - rise! __ The lit - tle red lark, Like a
Pulse of my heart, _ I pray! __ And out of thy hid - ing With

ONE SPRING MORNING

Ethelbert Nevin
(1862-1901)

Allegretto

One spring morn-ing bright and fair, Tra-la-la-la-la-la-la. ___

___ Roamed a shep-herd-ess and sang,

Tra-la-la-la-la-la-la. Young and beau-teous ___ free from care, ___

But as with the lambs, the scoff - er, Laughed at ___ hearts and ___

rib - bons too. Still ___ 'twas Tra - la - la - la - la - la, Tra - la - la - la - la - la,

più rit.   *a tempo*

Tra - la - la - la - la - la, Tra - la - la - la - la - la - la - la, Tra - la - la - la - la - la,

Tra - la - la - la - la - la, Tra - la - la - la - la - la - la.

THE ROSE HAS CHARMED THE NIGHTINGALE
(Plenívshis rósoi, salavyéi)

A. Koltzóff

English version by George Harris, Jr.
and Kurt Schindler

Nikolai Rimsky-Korsakov
(1844-1908)

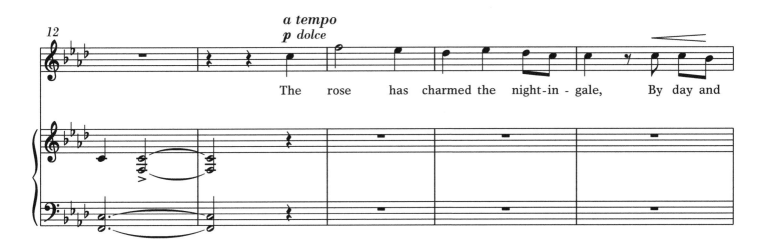

The rose has charmed the night-in-gale, By day and

night he tells the tale; The rose but hears in si - lent

won - der.

mf
Thus with his lyre a po - et sings To his young love most ten - der

p things; But oh! the maid can - not dis - cov - er For whom the song, nor

why his tune So sad - ly sounds be - neath the moon.

SONG OF LOVE

Music adapted from melodies of
Franz Schubert and Heinrich Berte
by Sigmund Romberg
(1887-1951)

Dorothy Donnelly

Once on a time, In a king-dom by the sea, Lived a young

prince sad and lone - ly, Un - der en - chant - ment of

sing - ing, bring - ing Se - crets sweet in its song to

me, Your vi - sion shines on me from a - bove,

You are my song of songs,

All the glo - ry of love.

STARS WITH GOLDEN SANDALS
(Sterne mit den gold'nen Füsschen)

Heinrich Heine
English version by Frederic Field Bullard

Robert Franz
(1815-1892)

Larghetto con grazia

Stars with lit-tle gold - en san-dals, Make your foot - steps soft __ and __ light Lest you wake the earth be - low you, Sleep-ing in __ the lap of night.

to Mrs. L.L. Krebs

TREES

Joyce Kilmer

Oscar Rasbach
(1888-1975)

I think that I shall nev-er

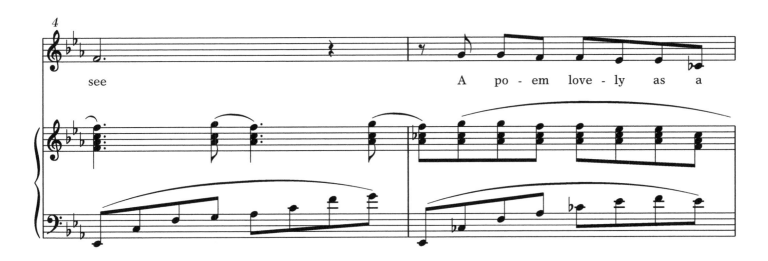

see

A po-em love-ly as a

tree.

A tree whose hun-gry mouth is

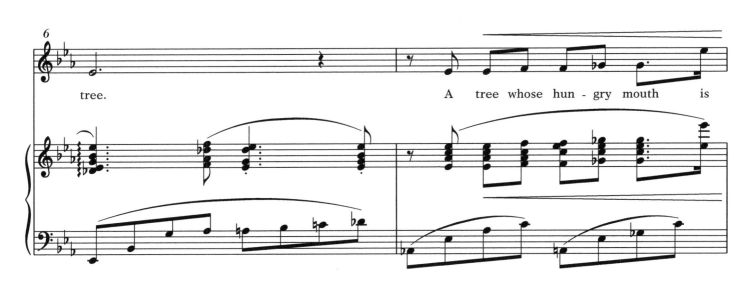

pressed _____ A - gainst the earth's sweet flow - ing breast; _____ A tree that looks at God all day, _____ And lifts her leaf - y arms to pray; A tree that may in sum-mer wear A nest of rob-ins in her

gradually faster

hair; Up - on whose bos - om snow has lain;

Who in - ti - mate - ly lives with rain. Po - ems are made by fools like

me, But on - ly God can make a tree.

dolce

8ba -

WAKE UP!
(Spring Flowers)

Montague F. Phillips
(1885-1969)

Harold Simpson